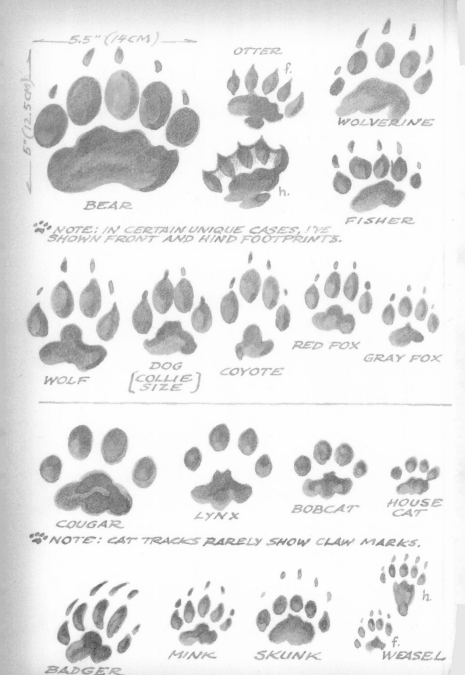

5.5" (14CM)

5" (12.5 cm)

OTTER f.

WOLVERINE

BEAR

h.

FISHER

NOTE: IN CERTAIN UNIQUE CASES, I'VE SHOWN FRONT AND HIND FOOTPRINTS.

WOLF

DOG [COLLIE SIZE]

COYOTE

RED FOX

GRAY FOX

COUGAR

LYNX

BOBCAT

HOUSE CAT

NOTE: CAT TRACKS RARELY SHOW CLAW MARKS.

BADGER

MINK

SKUNK

h.

f.

WEASEL

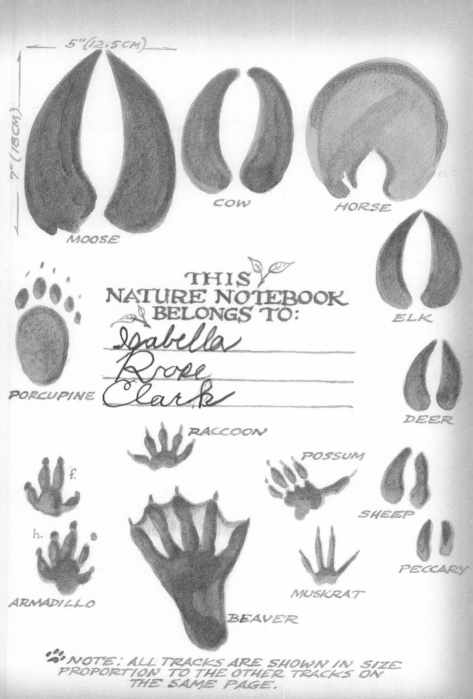

5"(12.5CM)

7"(18CM)

MOOSE

COW

HORSE

THIS
NATURE NOTEBOOK
BELONGS TO:

Isabella

Rose

Clark

ELK

PORCUPINE

DEER

RACCOON

POSSUM

f.

SHEEP

h.

ARMADILLO

BEAVER

MUSKRAT

PECCARY

NOTE: ALL TRACKS ARE SHOWN IN SIZE
PROPORTION TO THE OTHER TRACKS ON
THE SAME PAGE.

Library of Congress Cataloging-in-Publication Data
Arnosky, Jim.
Animal tracker / by Jim Arnosky.
p. cm. — (Jim Arnosky's nature notebooks)
SUMMARY: Presents tips on identifying animal tracks, with blank
pages provided for keeping records.
ISBN 0-679-86717-1
1. Animal tracks—Juvenile literature. [1. Animal tracks.
2. Nature study.] I. Title. II. Series: Arnosky, Jim.
Jim Arnosky's nature notebooks.
QL768.A74 1997 591'.0723—dc20 96-21644

Printed in the United States of America 10 9 8 7 6 5 4 3 2 1

JIM ARNOSKY'S
NATURE NOTEBOOKS

ANIMAL TRACKER

RABBIT TRACKS

Random House 🏠 New York

ANIMAL TRACKS

Did you know that it is possible to iden-
tify almost any animal from just one of
its footprints? Each species of animal has its
own unique foot shape. The footprints and
other marks made by mammals, birds, rep-
tiles, and insects as they move overland are
called animal tracks.

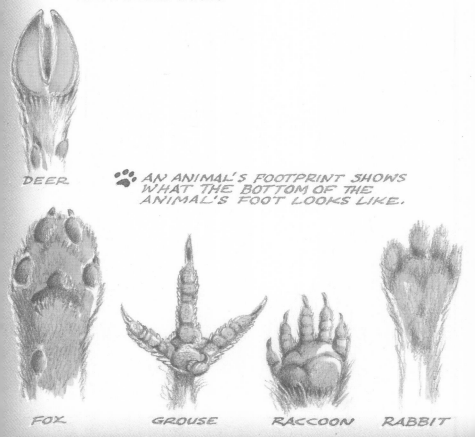

DEER

AN ANIMAL'S FOOTPRINT SHOWS
WHAT THE BOTTOM OF THE
ANIMAL'S FOOT LOOKS LIKE.

FOX   GROUSE   RACCOON   RABBIT

In warm seasons, look for animal tracks on wet beaches, shorelines, and moist woodland paths. In these places, the ground is soft enough to be imprinted by footsteps yet still firm enough to safely walk on. In dry or desert areas, look for animal tracks on dusty trails or in loose sand. In snow country, animal tracks are everywhere.

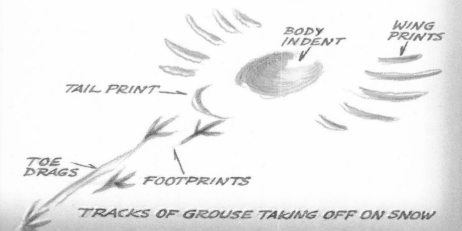

ONE ANIMAL CAN CREATE A VARIETY OF MARKS, ESPECIALLY IN SOFT SAND OR SNOW.

BODY INDENT

WING PRINTS

TAIL PRINT

TOE DRAGS

FOOTPRINTS

TRACKS OF GROUSE TAKING OFF ON SNOW

TRACK SETS

Whenever you find a single animal track, search the ground around it for other tracks to make the set. Tracks of birds and other two-footed animals consist of a right and left footprint. Tracks of four-footed animals include left and right front footprints and left and right hind footprints.

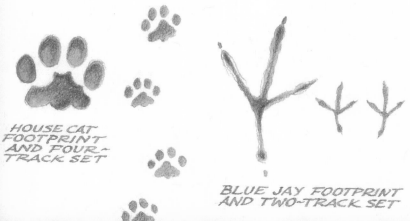

HOUSE CAT
FOOTPRINT
AND FOUR-
TRACK SET

BLUE JAY FOOTPRINT
AND TWO-TRACK SET

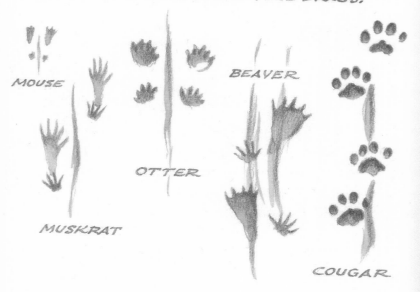

IN SNOW, SAND, OR MUD, SOME ANIMALS' TRACK SETS INCLUDE TAIL DRAGS.

MOUSE

BEAVER

OTTER

MUSKRAT

COUGAR

After you find one set of animal tracks, it is easy to locate another, and another, on the line of traveling tracks. Don't be tempted to follow. An animal's tracks may lead to unfamiliar surroundings and you could get lost. One complete set of tracks will tell you all you need to know.

PERFECT FOOTPRINTS

A single clearly pressed footprint can reveal the identity of the track-maker. And a complete set of tracks will show whether the animal was walking, running, hopping, sliding, or simply standing still.

WHEN FOUR—LEGGED ANIMALS HOP, JUMP, OR BOUND, THEIR HIND PRINTS REGISTER IN FRONT OF THE FRONT PRINTS ON EACH LANDING.

RABBIT TRACKS

WHEN I FIND TRACKS OF AN ANIMAL HOPPING, I LIKE TO MEASURE THE DISTANCE THE ANIMAL HOPPED.

10

STANDING TRACKS
ARE ALWAYS
FOLLOWED BY
MOTION TRACKS.

TRACKS OF A FOUR-LEGGED ANIMAL STANDING
STILL FORM A RECTANGLE OR A SQUARE.

IN WALKING TRACKS, THE FOOTPRINTS
ARE EVENLY SPACED IN TRACK SET AFTER SET.

TRACKS OF
AN ANIMAL
RUNNING ARE
CLOSELY SPACED
AND OFTEN SHOW
OVERPRINTING
OF FOOTPRINTS.

RUNNING TRACK
SETS ARE SPACED
A SMALL LEAP APART.

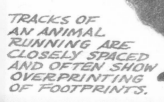

11

IDENTIFYING TRACKS

Some animals' tracks are uniquely shaped or fall in such a pattern that they can be identified at a glance. Deer hoofprints are heart-shaped. A raccoon's prints resemble tiny human hands and feet. Sets of fox tracks form straight dotted lines, and sets of striped-skunk tracks each form a neat diagonal line. All of these tracks are easily recognizable, especially in snow.

RACCOON TRACKS

STRIPED SKUNK TRACKS

DEER TRACKS

LINE OF FOX TRACKS IN SNOW

Other animals' tracks need to be studied more closely before they can be identified. Feline (the cat family) and canine (the dog family) footprints may look similar. But upon close inspection, you will see that because of their retractable claws, feline footprints are often missing toenail marks.

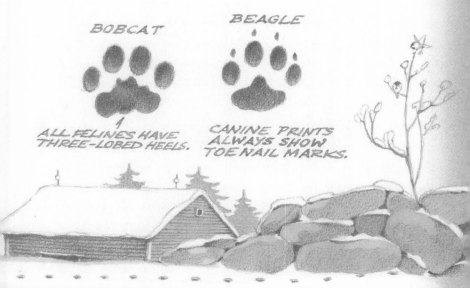

BOBCAT

BEAGLE

ALL FELINES HAVE THREE-LOBED HEELS.

CANINE PRINTS ALWAYS SHOW TOE NAIL MARKS.

TRACKING SAFETY

U sually by the time you discover an animal's tracks, the animal will be long gone. If, however, by some rare chance, you do see an animal at the end of its tracks, back away and leave the animal alone. Following on the heels of small animals causes them undue stress. And if cornered, even a small, harmless animal will defend itself.

ALLIGATOR TRACKS ON MUD

If your house happens to be in an area of the country where large, powerful animals such as alligators, bears, moose, or cougars are known to live, ask your parents to teach you how to recognize these animals' tracks, so if you ever happen to find such tracks, you will know immediately to stay clear of them.

RECORDING TRACKS

To record an animal's footprint in your notebook, make a small-scale sketch of the entire print. Be sure to show all toe and heel pads in their proper shape, size, and proportion. Then add any toenail marks. If the animal has hooves, sketch the hoof shape accurately. To record a whole set of tracks, draw a tiny diagram of the set showing each footprint in its precise placement in the set. In my notebooks, besides my sketches of animal tracks, I like to write down all the details of where and when I found the tracks.

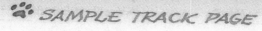

WHITE-TAILED DEER   JUNE 5, 1995

I WAS ON MY WAY TO THE POND
WHEN I SAW THE HOOFPRINTS
OF A DOE AND FAWN.

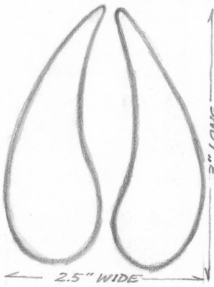

3" LONG

← 2.5" WIDE →
HOOFPRINT
IN SOFT SAND

12" STEPS

38" WALKING SET

FAWN TRACKS

1.75"

← 1.5" →

FAWN'S
PRINT

THE FAWN MUST HAVE BEEN
ONLY DAYS OLD. IT'S TRACKS
WERE SO TINY!

YOUR NATURE NOTEBOOK

Your nature notebook is small and flexible so you can roll it up, put it in a pocket, and carry it wherever you go. But as small as it may be, it can hold many wonderful experiences. Take care to write small and fit a lot on every page. Drawings of footprints, diagrams of track sets, tiny sketches of birds, bugs, and flowers you may see, along with a brief description of the time and place, can all fit on one or two notebook pages.

I'll be dropping in on a few more pages throughout the rest of the book to tell you a little more about animal tracks. Until then...

HAPPY TRACKS!

Jim Arnosky

A deer was
in Millorton
I saw some
Prints it looke
in heart shape
so it was a deer
print I think

3" Long

2.5" wide

Hoofprint it was a girl I am
in snow I'm not shore it it
was a fawn or a grown
up deer. I was near some
bushes near my house it Inn
asross the road.

Caroline Amanda and me found some dog tracks it was cool.

I saw a cat print in the ~~mad~~ House cat it was not fresh because nobody steped on the prints.

Collic Size

HOW FRESH IS THE TRACK?

It takes skill and practice to be able to accurately determine the freshness of an animal's tracks. The easiest way is to visit the same familiar spots day after day. You will quickly notice any new footprints that have been made since your last visit.

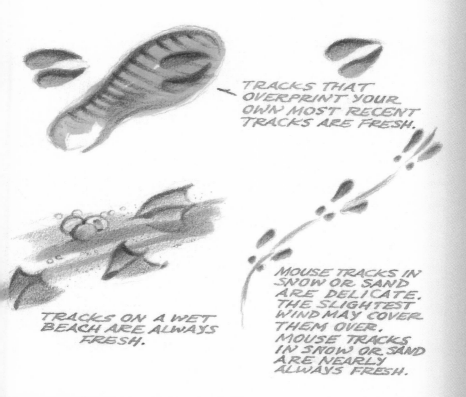

TRACKS THAT OVERPRINT YOUR OWN MOST RECENT TRACKS ARE FRESH.

MOUSE TRACKS IN SNOW OR SAND ARE DELICATE. THE SLIGHTEST WIND MAY COVER THEM OVER. MOUSE TRACKS IN SNOW OR SAND ARE NEARLY ALWAYS FRESH.

TRACKS ON A WET BEACH ARE ALWAYS FRESH.

Crab

mina

Seagull

☙ ABOUT DEWCLAWS

MANY MAMMALS HAVE DEWCLAWS—THE SMALL TOES HIGH UP ON THE FEET.

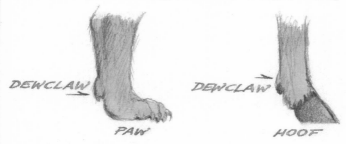

DEWCLAW →

PAW

DEWCLAW →

HOOF

☙ IN PAWED ANIMALS, DEWCLAWS ARE MOSTLY FUNCTIONLESS AND THEY RARELY SHOW IN TRACKS.

☙ HOOFED ANIMALS USE THEIR DEWCLAWS FOR ADDED STABILITY WHEN WALKING ON ICE, MUD, IN DEEP SNOW, AND WHEN RUNNING AT GREAT SPEED. DURING THESE TIMES, DEWCLAWS REGISTER IN TRACKS, DIRECTLY BEHIND HOOFPRINTS.

MOOSE TRACKS IN MUD

DEER RUNNING HARD

AS SNOW MELTS, ANIMAL TRACKS PRINTED
IN THE SNOW ENLARGE AND BECOME
VERY DISTORTED.

DOG TRACKS BEGIN TO RESEMBLE TRACKS
OF WOLVES OR BEARS.

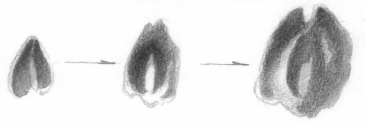

DEER TRACKS ENLARGE AND LOOK MORE
LIKE MOOSE TRACKS.

AND SETS OF RABBIT TRACKS MELT TOGETHER
AND SUGGEST GIANT FOOTPRINTS.

🐾 CONSIDER HOW MUCH A TRACK
HAS MELTED AND ENLARGED
BEFORE CONCLUDING THAT
"BIGFOOT" IS IN YOUR TOWN.

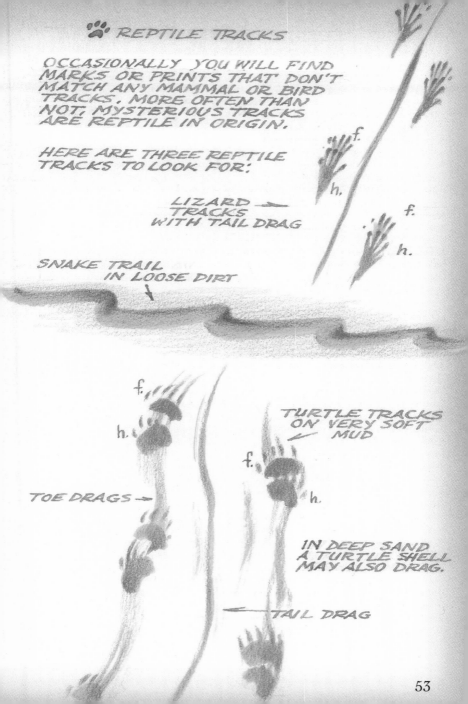

REPTILE TRACKS

OCCASIONALLY YOU WILL FIND MARKS OR PRINTS THAT DON'T MATCH ANY MAMMAL OR BIRD TRACKS. MORE OFTEN THAN NOT, MYSTERIOUS TRACKS ARE REPTILE IN ORIGIN.

HERE ARE THREE REPTILE TRACKS TO LOOK FOR:

LIZARD TRACKS WITH TAIL DRAG →

f.

h.

f.

h.

SNAKE TRAIL IN LOOSE DIRT

f.

h.

TURTLE TRACKS ON VERY SOFT MUD

f.

h.

TOE DRAGS →

IN DEEP SAND A TURTLE SHELL MAY ALSO DRAG.

← TAIL DRAG

ABOUT THE AUTHOR

Naturalist Jim Arnosky has written and illustrated over 35 nature books for children. His titles have earned numerous honors, including American Library Association Notable Book Awards and Outstanding Science Books for Children Awards presented by the National Science Teachers Association Children's Book Council Joint Committee. He has also received the Eva L. Gordon Award for Body of Work for his contribution to children's literature.

An all-around nature lover, Mr. Arnosky can often be found fishing, hiking, boating, or videotaping wildlife on safari. He lives with his family in South Ryegate, Vermont.

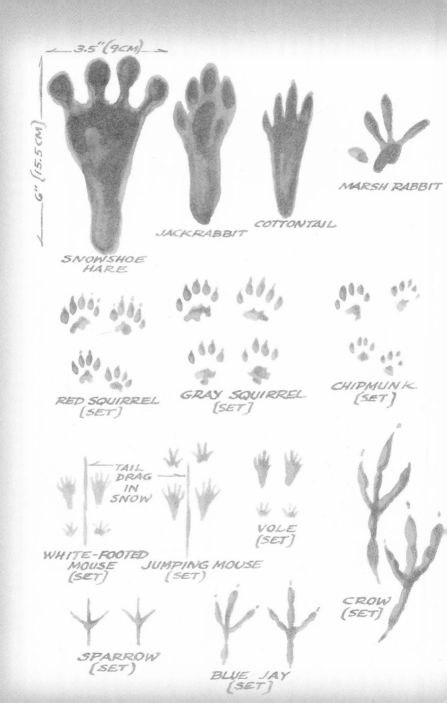

3.5" (9CM)

6" (15.5CM)

SNOWSHOE HARE

JACKRABBIT

COTTONTAIL

MARSH RABBIT

RED SQUIRREL (SET)

GRAY SQUIRREL (SET)

CHIPMUNK (SET)

TAIL DRAG IN SNOW

WHITE-FOOTED MOUSE (SET)

JUMPING MOUSE (SET)

VOLE (SET)

CROW (SET)

SPARROW (SET)

BLUE JAY (SET)

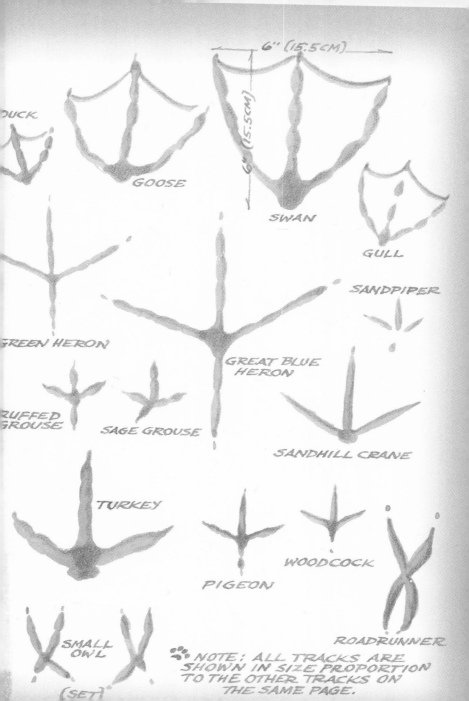

DUCK

GOOSE

6" (15.5CM)

6" (15.5CM)

SWAN

GULL

GREEN HERON

SANDPIPER

GREAT BLUE HERON

RUFFED GROUSE

SAGE GROUSE

SANDHILL CRANE

TURKEY

PIGEON

WOODCOCK

SMALL OWL

(SET)

ROADRUNNER

NOTE: ALL TRACKS ARE SHOWN IN SIZE PROPORTION TO THE OTHER TRACKS ON THE SAME PAGE.